JO D'ARC

Jo D'a produ based in Glasgow, where she is also a passionate community worker and activist. Originally hailing from Dunfermline in Fife, Jo began writing at a young age. She was forever scribbling poems, lyrics or stories on scraps of paper or the back of her hand. Grounded in music, Jo has begun to experiment with her writing, bringing her storytelling from those scraps of paper into the world of written and spoken word.

Jo sings and plays bass guitar in alternative art-punk band **The Twistettes** and social-commentary-fuelled dystopian gutter rock act **Girobabies**. She can also be found behind the decks DJ'ing techno/electro music as **DJ Jo D'arc** or cranking out sassy soul, doo-wop and pristine pop as **Jo Jive and the B-Hive 5**.

Jo's latest musical incarnation is experimental electronic project **Minerva Wakes**, which sits somewhere between lush trip-hop and gritty dubstep. The debut album 'Mirrored Moon' is the musical embodiment of the story published here.

This pamphlet is part of a multi-artform project that combines music, photography, poetry and prose to tell the tale of the goddess Minerva's awakening. To explore other aspects of the project or to check out Jo's other work, visit jodarc.co.uk.

Minerva and the Whir

by

Jo D'arc

Cover artwork by Jo D'arc

Thanks to Victoria McNulty and Lucy Tertia George for
editing and encouragement.

Wordville
www.wordville.net
info@wordville.net

Contents

Minerva and the Whir 1

Minerva Wakes 20

She Dances 23

Clay Mounds 24

Or Rather 25

A Rainbow Trickles 26

As We Turn 27

Only Flow 28

Minerva and the Whir

I

Minerva has slept for many thousands of years. In a trance, she glides and slithers, creeps and jolts, dancing with light between her fingers like golden grains of sand. In her agile slumber, a faint scent begins to emerge. She is slowly filled with the treacle-thick smell of earth and flowers. Smell is always the first sense to go at the end of a journey and, equally, is the first to come back on arrival at a new destination. It is like a springboard for the rest, a cue to draw.

She tries to stay floating on ether, but it becomes harder and harder to maintain. She is pulled and pulped. She feels energy moving and massaging her from head to toe and as it forcefully kneads her knots, it extracts her further. Before she knows it, she is crashing through caverns and down rabbit holes. She tries to make sense of it all, but everything is moving so fast now, and she can't grab a single thought. Yet she knows that she must.

Up from the earth's core she is squeezed through stalagmites and mounds of hanging rock. She passes by worms and grubs as they weave their homes from the land. The process of unravelling is dense and pressurised. All she has ever been flashes through her. Good, bad, neutral, and every tiny nuance that differentiates or connects this three-sided coin. She feels them all. She weeps and coils and embraces herself, impossible to know how long she has been in this state of flux and endurance.

A rumbling pressure is slowly building, pushing her down, reducing her mass, making her small. If she had not experienced this a million times before she would swear that one of the bold boys of the heavens, maybe Jupiter or Juno, was pacing around in her metaphorical bedroom, minimising her to maximise themselves. They don't realise that to boost one is to boost all. No matter how bright a candle burns it can't extinguish another. Her understanding of this is the reason she is the ultimate.

She knows that this reducing motion is all of her own conduction. Something in her wants to be compressed. To be solid. As she condenses, she is aware of her returning strength. Power-harnesses and hones as matter emerges. Lucidity swells her attention, reaching from the pulse of her core. The eternal beat of everything. The beat we all dance to. Including Jupiter and Juno. The beat of the beat.

II

The act of taking human form is not for the faint-hearted. It's an incredibly long process that ultimately serves to enforce the simplicity of the human essence on an untameable, unfathomable entity. Various manoeuvres of consciousness tear and pummel till uncertainty and confusion forms a low-level hum that allows Minerva to engage on this earthly plane. Alongside this hum sits a perfect fifth of eternal striving. The harmonics of this sound aren't apparent to the human ear, but the wider universe can hear the discord. A cycle of perpetual effort, forever searching for the answer. The meaning. The heart of the matter.

This hum very often leads to humans missing the point. For them, on top of these notes ring layer upon layer of incoherent noise, adding to their confusion. Frequencies of beauty and beast combine and warp into one energy dense pounding Whir. Constant worry about who they are and what this means. Constant questions of 'does that sound like something I would say?', 'is this something I would do?', and the eternal fashion quandary, 'is this outfit really "me"?' For lifetimes, humans wish away what they have, focusing on what they want next instead of where they are now.

To be human is to sink into a beautiful velvet-drenched bed while focusing on the unreachable clouds above. As striving mortals always do, they alter their consciousness and become sewn together in attachment in furious pursuit of the answer. Or, more frequently, in fearful concern that there is no answer. Preoccupied by pushing and doing and living, they do none of these effectively at all.

In brief moments, people do relax and forget, letting time unravel them. Watching that cloud slowly float by while indulging in a velour glow instead of striving to catch what they don't need to reach. In these moments there is a glimmer of understanding. Human minds spark with the energy of a thousand worlds and breathe in time with the rhythm of the trees. Whether or not they have sight, or even eyes, it is possible for humankind to still see with a clarity that defines dreams. Despite this, they are always swept back into the cycle that has spun since birth was birthed. Striving, impatient and filled with exacerbated excess effort as they chant 'come on, come on, come on'.

III

As the intensity of her transformation dissipates, Minerva slowly becomes aware of her human body. She circles a wrist and shakes out her long hair, finding her feet directly below her knees as they should be. Suddenly, in a bubble of sound, she begins to listen. A rising sense of curiosity bursts through her veins alongside a vague sense of looming unease. Despite being fully aware that curiosity is a great downfall of the human species, she indulges. 'What has happened here?' she asks.

Her growing concept of time and space tells her things have changed. She feels a buzz, a vibration that she is altogether unfamiliar with. The Whir. It seems the Whir is something of a different beast than when she last danced with it. Born of a mass assimilation of energy and connections spanning the entire world, it grows daily. The volume and intensity are now quite something.

New technologies have increased the ferocity far more than she had ever considered possible. Progressive thoughts and joyous momentum can now be shared as readily as war cries and humdrum. The world is connected in an instant, forever building and layering. Connection without need for touch or even presence. And mere humans did this. Minerva is astounded. Her interest is peaked. How delightful.

Basking in the new frequency, diving and dallying, she runs fingers through sticky strands of engagement, indulging so ferociously that her heart begins to shake and bubble. These bubbles hint that she should step back for a moment, but she can't. Enamoured by the all-consuming magnitude of what has been created, she is in awe of her people. She feels love expand from deep within. Forgetting her human format, she lets it soar.

And then suddenly, an explosion. Dramatic flumes of gold burst from her body rupturing into a luminous mushroom cloud. The sound rumbles and momentarily slices through the fizzing connections of the Whir. The aftershock jolts with such aggressive intent that it causes the earth to tilt and spin on a new axis, creating waves of magnitude from sky to sky. Minerva is instantly full of remorse for her disruptive intrusion on the beautiful beam of hopeful illusion she had basked in just moments earlier. She scolds herself lightly, chiding that she is now in a body and must act accordingly.

As she absentmindedly moulds a new beating heart she wonders if the Whir can sense her. Can it sense itself? Does it feel the depths of her? Did it see her morphing as she flailed in the fizz of limbo between 'being' and 'living'? Had it felt her heart explode? She must know. 'Tell Me' she projects to the stars in a ruminating mantra.

IV

In great sweeps Minerva moves. She stirs ponds and lochs letting them know she is home again. She blows gentle questions into the wind, revelling in its movement. Gleefully, she rides the soft waves her effort creates and, as she flows in the breeze, the air infuses her body in a gentle swooshing swoop.

Gaining momentum, Minerva's intensifying light deep dives from a window on the side of the moon. Hurtling to the ground it changes shade to match its peers. Greys, blues, greens, browns then oranges and reds give way to a tar black at the centre of this universe that then catapults her back up through the molten core of the earth's soul. Scorched and exhilarated, her light rebounds through her forehead. Like the eternally exhausted turtle, tired from the everlasting effort and perseverance it takes to hold up the entire world, the light infuses Minerva with knowledge as it strains with the weight of the world's woes. Simmering and forlorn, it twists its way into Minerva's psyche. And, as the turtle burrows, the wind tells tales.

Tales are tattled of the fantastic and ferocious energetic Whir. As a swirling throng of heightened human reverb, it reflects all. The world is connected like never before. Knowledge is disseminated as freely as it ever has and at an unprecedented pace. There is no one filter; there are many. It is chaos in all its splendour and savagery. Humans can know all or nothing within the haze of a lazy

Sunday afternoon. In days gone by this could only ever have been imagined by Goddesses and Gods. Yet now, everyone can indulge. Even a person drenched in life can access a little of the Goddess-like glow, so powerful this reverberation is.

A tender touch can be projected through time and space without strain. Communities have formed that foster growth and tend to higher callings. Yet, with this exquisite expanse also comes manual actions and marks. A punch can be felt boldly on the other side of the world and its impact bounces and lands to a different beat. Off kilter rhythms lead to torture and the echo of the dismissed and diminished goes unaddressed. The Whir is magnificent yet terrifying in its anarchic lurches and lulls.

Minerva hears all and despite the growing gnaw of dismay beginning to grow low in her gut, she is still drawn to the vibration; she wants to play. Maybe her presence will bring change for the better, she contemplates, as she is drawn back to surf the waves of this human hum. She wriggles and swoops while stomping out moves. She bangs her drum and unites her beat with the Whir.

The wind sweeps forth in frustration knocking Minerva off balance. It sees why she dances. It sees the joy in this miracle of creation. It sees the vision that carries Minerva and takes her away. Fooling her into thinking she can connect. It is a youthful powerhouse of intrigue formed from nothing and by nobody. It has the eyes of a beauty coming of age, awash with innocent altruism yet layered with ulterior intent. Minerva is drawn down, giggling as she plunges. With a tug of something like jealousy, the wind whispers under its breath, 'the Whir may bring joy now but soon you will see her true rhythm.'

The Whir does not hold the knowledge of millennia as the wind does. It is juvenile and cannot even begin to be the answer Minerva needs. The Whir can only see itself and images of itself. It reflects what it thinks is truth and manufactures a dance that imitates this. The dance fuels a beat and, as you move a hip or a leaf, a symphony of drums erupts. But this is not real. It's all backwards. The world turned upside down. You may feel fucking fantastic when in its grip, but it can't be sustained. It is hollow.

Despite all this, the Whir has many facets and can create a lustrous façade of pretty pigmented plastic whenever needed. It resembles good and can be truly serene. But it can also be serpent-like.

Warning Minerva, the wind whispers, 'if you lose your guard, you lose your mind.' Minerva scoffs at the drama of the air, breathing beyond its station. There is an ancient strength in the breeze. It knows Minerva's frivolous side and insists to be heard. It must communicate that the Whir can blow the mind clean out of any body, even that of a Goddess, if its owner becomes too lost in its contradictions.

From nowhere, flutes and clarinets muster sounds that break the lusty hold of the Whir in one pitch perfect soar of music. The sound glides around the entire universe ringing as a reminder to Minerva of her recent loss of heart. It coaxes her to understand that even the great Goddess can be tarnished by the superfluously sculpted scripts of the Whir. In frustration, the wind blows even harder till no other in existence can air a tone or tune. And, this time, Minerva hears.

V

Finally, taking heed, Minerva leaves the Whir. She still feels the hum, but she deflects its delight, summoning her own vibration to drown it out with the pulse of a she-drum. The Goddess takes to her feet and walks the world barefoot till she has seen it all. She lets the soil fill her with the story of her absence. Absorbing the atmosphere, centring her spine, she lingers, leers, luxuriates and laments.

The birds and lions and sea nymphs and fairies tell her stories of blood-battled crusades and captured slaves. Her feet meet the soil and, with every step, she lives a lifetime. Sharp bolts of emotion and lived experience crack her soul violently. She is the pain of the disengaged. She is the toil of the poor. She is the fury of the dismissed. She feels herself slowly fill with a gory sense of incivility. This is not the point. This is not your point.

Minerva lets out a cry that sends a ripple of air out in all directions. As she does this the wind circles uncontrollably in a spiral that sucks the life from every patch of earth it touches. In response, the sun is charged and fires up with concern, illuminating case after case where humans got it right. Minerva stops in her tracks. Tilting her head to the sun she lets its rays massage her face with hope. Just as she was about to reach the point where she could take no more of the brutal revelations of the clay, she is given reprieve.

The sun shines with the joy of giving and helping. The spirits of those propelled to good despite having no gain in doing so are illuminated and held high. The gravelly determination of those who stand up and challenge when others are unable to is shone upon. The sun, Sol, reminds her of the blissful moments she spent playing with the new bold Whir of energy. Sol reflects to her that she was close to enveloping the joy of the Whir. Sol shines on the love

Minerva felt at the discovery of her prodigy's buzz. The manifestation of all earthly actions. There is so much good.

Yet, the mud and rock draw her back, lambasting her energy with grim and selfish deeds repeated and repeated and repeated. Selfish men and irreverent leaders. So much skill and wisdom carved up in terror and used for wrong. She holds onto her new heart as it pounds and aches. Eventually, escaping the chime of all who need to communicate to her, Minerva runs for an eternity till she is lost.

VI

As Minerva wanders in the world, with no want to find her way, she stumbles through towns and marketplaces. Broken pathways lead to obscured doorways. Beautifully sculpted gardens expand to unveil mansions with brightly painted gates. Taverns split at the seams with pints of fun and fear. Advertisements line the streets. Women with faces looking blown and contorted sit beside men with flesh moulded in a way in which nature would never sign off. This is beauty? A billboard stretches the length of an entire street advertising the 'best entertainment system in the world.' It displays bold images of humans shooting and maiming each other in brutal detail. With each murky step the blood drains from Minerva's face.

She falters in disbelief as a large man walks past with human flesh suits on a rack. The sight makes her stomach flip even more violently than it did when she had unwittingly walked into a cow carcass hung in the street for people to peel pieces off one by one. She follows the large man, wondering what on earth he could be planning to do with his collection. They round a corner, and he stops outside a shop. It quickly becomes apparent he is selling.

'PRICE NEGOTIABLE', a large sign reads. 'Spend a night in the perfectly preserved skin of a beautiful young woman or strong young man of your choice.' 'Don't dream, just do.' It goes on, 'All skin is expertly treated and engineered so you can truly experience life as the most beautiful and intoxicating version of you.' Despite an instinctive internal recoiling, Minerva approaches the man and asks where he got his skins.

He switches into sales mode and guides her to a rack which, he tells her, is just what she needs. He begins his pitch. 'This is from a lovely stock of ladies from the far north. Hand-reared and fed only the very best organic food. Selectively bred for three generations now...' His words phase in and out as she strokes the soft skin of a particularly beautiful suit. With every touch she feels the life of its owner. The despair and dread she lived with, the torture of captivity and knowing how her fate would be met. Minerva bites her lip to stifle a tear.

Admiring the blaze of deep red hair which she twirls between her fingers, Minerva has a fleeting thought. She wonders how this suit could transform her own raven locks. How it may help her be a better version of 'her'. Would she feel more powerful? Would she have more fun? Would it make life that bit easier if she became an auburn beauty? She shakes off this protruding rumination, disgusted with herself for indulging in such a thought, cursing the Whir for sucking her into its dark chasm-like grasp yet again.

She knows this man is a hustler and will manipulate her into believing she needs this suit at all costs. She knows this skin has been ripped mercilessly from the back of someone too poor to keep the beauty she was born with. It seems, in this world, it is only those who have money and possessions who may enjoy this level of aesthetic perfection. Minerva muses gravely that this must be to hide the rotting, stinking core of it all.

VII

It is here that Minerva first uses her powers to intervene in the world. She interrupts the man's sales pitch and curses him. 'May you forever be trampled by those whom you have trampled for your own ends.' She clicks her fingers and unlocks the past momentarily. In the fleeting instants in which all of time melds, Minerva reunites the women from the far north with their suits and they roar in giddy delight as they feel comfortable back in their own skin. With another click of her fingers, every other skin suit is reunited with its rightful owner. In a blaze of human-like joy, Minerva glints.

The man is also mutated but his fate is to be a grim one. His skin is stolen from his body in the same cruel manor he has tortured many before. With an iron grip, his skin is stretched out as far and wide as the edges of the universe. He feels every winch as it pulls his skin tighter and tighter. With a third click of her fingers, Minerva instantly cuts the man's skin into hundreds of pairs of shoes for those mistreated by him. Forever they would trample him. Every day, as they walk and dance and leap, the man will feel the pain of being stamped down, undermined and left in the dirt.

At this point, Minerva does reflect that an eye for an eye is not how an enlightened being should behave and such an act lays question to her intent, morality and even her enlightenment. Questions always need to be posed, especially to those with as much power as the Goddess. If no questions are asked, then great tragedies occur.

Having been without their skin for so long, they all have an appreciation for things just as they are. They dance and sing and fall in love, revelling in the wonder of being.

Some of the suits were damaged from maltreatment or mistakes. Yet, those who ended up with kinks or wonks in their skin are just so happy to have skin at all that they rejoice regardless and embrace imperfection in themselves and others wholeheartedly.

Some people accidentally end up in another's skin on initial transition. The joy of acceptance meant that with some investigation and soul seeking, they could easily find the skin that was meant for them so they could feel at home and comfortable. The ecstasy of being in their own skin and being proud of that is so powerful that other humans start to apply this to their interpretation of their image. Elation spreads through the Whir.

Purring as Minerva indulges it, the Whir pulls her close enough to touch. Minerva's energy splinters into millions of pieces which are distributed to humans worldwide through the churn of the Whir. As Minerva relaxes into this, she feels a tugging. She is being pulled in all directions, at first gently and respectfully and then ferociously. The Whir is sucking her in.

As she adjusts her stance, attempting to gather herself Minerva hears the clang of a million coins. They rain on her from all around, spinning in circles until they fall tinkering at her feet. As she gains focus, she realises there has been some kind of awakening caused by the cascading of her earlier shattered energy. The Whir is buzzing with the collective acknowledgement of the Goddess's presence. Dismayed by her loss of anonymity, she reasons that this may be what is needed for human consciousness to evolve. Maybe they will use her energy to heal.

The rich and powerful are besieging her with offers of jewels and gold, throwing coins at her feet. 'What do they ask for?' Minerva wonders, intrigued. Intrigue turns to irritation as it become clear that although they pretend otherwise, the act of giving is not out of respect or even adoration. It is not a call for her to help the misfortunate. They throw money to beg that she give them more; to provide yet more abundance for those who can already mine all the precious stones they could ever desire. Yet, they ask for nothing for those who hold not a single jewel.

Surely, they can't be serious? Untangling herself she disconnects again. Enraged by this lack of understanding she cuts the Whir off with a roar. 'Don't you try to buy me. What I am cannot be bought with all the riches of the world.'

VIII

Saddened and worn down by her recent interaction with humans, Minerva questions her motives for getting involved. It's still not clear to her why she has manifest in this form again. She is beginning to notice that the Whir is evoking an increasingly uneasy feeling in her core. This incessant gnawing is fuelled further still by the renewed chatter of the elements that found her soon after she started playing about with time and reality. It seems this is not the best move when trying to stay lost.

Minerva knows what to do to soothe this edgy feeling. She must dance. It may not be an instant fix, but it will start the process of conjuring inspiration. As soon as she decides this, she hears the swell of drums. Moving through streets and pathways she finds herself drawn to nature. She swings her hips, limbering up to move her body as she finds music in a glen filled with pine trees and honeybees. She stomps and jives, creating circles and losing control of limbs as they lasso through the air. Wildness takes over her thought-broken mind, processing nothing but the beat. Her beat.

Hours pass as she dances with fever, letting go and connecting all at once. When she finally opens her eyes, a boy stands across from her. He is playing a drum, pounding out his beat while dancing as boldly as Minerva. Her eyes flicker with interest. One of the poignancies of being in a body is enjoying the full expression of this in all its creative sways and wild throes of passion. She runs a hand down her chest, lingering around her navel then moves down further yet. She pins the boy's eyes with hers and starts to dance towards him. He reciprocates with an animalistic grunt and they are in each other's arms. Minerva is strong and agile, and the boy is a fair match. As they move together Minerva loses her beat and in a frenzy of love she twists and turns to the boy's drum, feeling every sound. They tussle and play, loving each other in the most intense way. Afterwards, they lay in each other's arms telling secrets and sharing laughs.

Suddenly the boy stands, preparing to leave. Minerva follows and asks when they will meet again. The boy evasively shrugs this off saying he will be in touch. Minerva flushes with a mix of hurt and shame. Maybe he will? His tone said otherwise. Being a supreme being affords Minerva a certain psychic ability. Although this has not been fully honed in her current human form, it still works. Her sixth sense tells her the boy had not felt what she had. In fact, it seems the boy may have tricked her. She stamps a foot as she realises her reason for dancing had been lost when she melded with him. As beautiful as the moment was, she now finds herself alone, frustrated and no further forward.

IX

Feeling shunned and suddenly lacking in confidence in her own intuition, Minerva takes to the road again. She feels a rumbling of intent inside but doesn't have the conviction to act on it. In fact, she is so deflated that she can't even bring herself to acknowledge that she has some greater purpose here. But, with each step, her heart bounces back a little further into her chest until, eventually, she is able to feel at ease again.

As dusk sets, Minerva stops to build a camp for the night in a clearing beside a slow-flowing river. As she fashions a vibrant bed of orange and yellow out of autumn leaves, she touches her chest and feels the beat of her heart. 'This is my heart, and I will not give it so easily again, and certainly not to a drummer with bold hips who is hanging around making music in a field all summer.' She knows that the trauma of living and re-living the mistakes and blunders of hapless humanity has weakened her and sent her down a spiral of poor decisions. This is her time to reset.

Minerva moves toward the river to wash her face. She looks at the water, gazes at its movement with appreciation and hears its babbles. Then she sees her own face. A perfect reflection of her dark wild hair and wide eyes. As she stares at herself, her face pulsing through the water, it becomes crystal clear what she must do. She suddenly understands her path. Her purpose this time is set in her veins, surging with intent as it has all the other times she has materialised. This knowledge never rises from an external source; it is always from the beat of her own drum. She always knew what she needed to know, she just needed to remember she knew it.

As her awareness gains momentum, Minerva can see her beat rise from the pulse in the water. She begins to move again. It starts from her heart and pounds progressively out, banging on bones and muscle till it finds a steady streaming rhythmic flow. She does not need someone to create this beat for her or even to drum along with her. She makes her own rhythm, and it fuels her energy, creating nuances in notes and limitless assertions that she is and she knows.

Minerva knows one of the joys of creating connections is the motion of joining her beat with another. But true magic happens when beats can go solo and one feels whole doing so. These rhythms will always seek each other out and will always strengthen and infuse each other. Lovers, friends and family all bang their own distinct drum while also entwining in a beautiful synchronicity with the souls they seek out. Your rhythm will always connect you to you. It will change you, break you, move you forward to adventures and highs. Listening to her own drum, Minerva arrives.

X

The babbling becomes more pronounced till stories are formed in the flow of the river as Minerva kneels by the edge of the water. She stands and follows the riverbank, crashing through mighty waterfalls and softly tip–toeing over ice. Though in some incarnations water can be unforgiving, there is a fluidity in its nature that means it will forever see all sides and be able to come and go with each varied opinion. This is what ultimately builds such strength.

In response to Minerva's dismay at the humans' ways, the water nymphs and creatures again emphasis the good to be seen in humans. 'I have bathed with many a human who was almost entirely selfless,' exclaims one nymph. Another chimes in to protest that 'many only reap what they need while giving away much more than they have sewn.' The bubbles of the burn cluster to support this, intent that humans are not a lost cause. In fact, with some work, the river ventures, 'they could be the most exquisitely thoughtful and beautiful beings in the full universe.'

Yet, the doorway to the soul is through the sole and, despite water's majesty, it is clay that has the final say. The earth connects all elements, touching each just enough to have as close to the whole picture as is possible. And the gravel is unconvinced. Silt-rallied energy binds in tight knots and ignites through Minerva's being. As this happens the last piece of the puzzle falls into place and Minerva now knows. She is serene in her knowing. Her heartbeat is steady. She feels her breath move in and out through her nose. The calm before she storms.

Minerva takes one last look around, sweeping the entire universe with one quick glance and then she begins to peel back the layers of human bone and gristle. Cracking and fractured, her teeth clench as the intensity of her power is unleashed. The hum of the Whir is overwhelmed in seconds. The notion that Minerva even entertained the Whir as an entity seems utterly ridiculous now. Sounds and visuals merge to create a sweeping mass of destruction. Noise envelopes all that is, as light crescendos in spikes of metal on metal.

The last human feature to implode is Minerva's spine which stretches out to all corners of the world till it encases the atmosphere. Everything goes still for a simple second and then a swift tug of her spinal cord shatters the illusion as the fabric of the universe tumbles down. Sound begins to subside and light floats in beams of nothingness. This gently simmers as time unfolds completely, leaving no concept or meaning. No thoughts. No effort. No winners. No anger. No talent. Nothing.

XI

Back to inception. Minerva is. We all are. Pulled back into the only hum that is eternal. The only vibration. We are all part of a beautiful, unbeatable, perfect soul. We have no concept of time or space and this brings happiness. Not only to those of us who have an inability to adapt to a time-based existence and are perpetually late for everything, but for everyone. Because we are one.

Nobody is rushing to go somewhere because we are already here. Nobody is striving to beat anyone because we all win. Nobody is trying to hurt anyone because we all hurt. To reach or strive is to scream into the void. And that is pointless. Minerva simply holds us till everything is still again. We are complete. We are whole. We are.

Maybe these occasional screams into the abyss are actually glitches that sometimes create bubbles and these bubbles sometimes become universes and these universes sometimes create life similar to that of the humans in this tale.

Or, maybe, that's just a suitably odd way to end this weird wee story.

Poetry

by

Jo D'arc

MINERVA WAKES

I

Minerva wakes from a slumber deep in silt
She moves and sways, bound and grazed as her gaze
inflates
She begins to create sound and jilts the wormholes the
world expects her to move through to come alive

Unspoken and strange
She invades

A strong arm stretches
Muscle flexed with a gentle grasp as energy spirals
From cocoon she reaches and is reached in one spinning
flow
Retched and effervescent in equal measures she pulses,
prickles and perspires

She is preceptor of her path
She is real
Yet she is illusory
She builds and hones and while chiselling bones

She slowly unfolds

II

Minerva's essence flinches as she steps forth through boulders and slime
Her first breath of air, laced with soil and gold, takes her there
She digs her feet into the ground below and feels
The wind whispers through a haze of shattered glass and as it reaches her ears; its reverberation is piercing

She pauses
then a lone sharp inhalation

A tear falls from her earth-laden eye as she asks. What has happened here?

As the earth and wind chime incessantly all around
Her form is firming and soul burning in equal amplification
Tattles and tales of monstrous acts of greed under the guise of civilization echo as her core cracks
She rips open her throat and shrieks into the night sky with such urgency that the sun rises instantly
Flares of hope fire in the distance, flames licking her toes as she strides out into the world
But despite this glimmer, all she feels is that the toil and drill of self-interest obsessively prevails
Her fruit has ripened beyond control, mutated and corrupt

She is lost

III

Leaping over rocks to meet the lapping waves
Her last hope is to be assured that there is good here

The sea swings in circles
Mild natured spirits inhabit this space and they have a true
want to save the humans' grace
Yarning pictures of sacrifice and kindhearted vice, liquid
motions evoke anecdotes of song that lifts the spirit and
unites
Despite the wider woe

But no matter how the river tries
her feet remain planted on clay that tells her from sole up
how she must sway

As extreme as her awakening, her spine now entwines in a
coil of zeal pulled from every nook
Through wild hair and bold eyes she ignites
Florescent light spikes like multifaceted sheets of pearl
Her teeth clench as she summons everything that 'is' back
to her breast

As time disintegrates, her form gently implodes
And with this, unequivocal love is restored

We are back to inception

She Dances

Rewind the box
Shapes explode
Casting innocent flairs in side streets bare
Plumes of colour carnival with brazen eyes
Bold with beauty and barrels of pride

Unfolding
Engrossing
Enchanting
Exposing

Slip on glittering gilded glass
An irreverent step takes a severed path
Colours drip grey down cheeks thick with chances
Irreverent become irrelevant as magic winds the ballerina
And she dances

Clay Mounds

Up from the earth clay mounds make sound
They move to a beat, feet to feet
With unstuck steps they cling to that yin
Sliding souls glide with ticking minds
Back to their kin

One thousand strokes a brush invokes
One hundred flutters as a butterfly utters
Cut up yet connected, at war yet invested
Steady legs draw patterns
As sand and soot stand hand in hand

Swirling maps pull us in
Through roots still planted with an earthy grin
As time moves on, these feet soften and need shin
Yet bare feet always know
Despite the drippings of a conspiring snow

While one burns, another bathes
As if to balance the endless day
Forever moving through an awe inspired illusion
Actions, words, grooves, musings
Sometimes pretty and sometimes gruesome

Yet however the pin flings we still simply long to climb back
into each other
Leaves of silver dissolve into the tree mother
Every single rustle feels real and right
And even in spite
Eventually, clay mounds re-unite

Or Rather

In the mirror
Lost in eyes
Glued they imply
Cells clump and multiply

Creeping mass
Organic matter
That is me
Or rather
That is my father

Waves and bumps
Curls and lumps
Expand, contract, ignite
Too bright

Dim light, opaque night
The stage of my fight
This is me
Or rather
This is my mother

Toes to nose
I am exposed
Look for what is
On the edge of this fizz

In desire to feel
Something, yet nothing
I see I am me
Or rather
I am my artist

A Rainbow Trickles

A rainbow trickles from brow to chin
Covers contours of convention with a flick of vim
Maps woven from veins and blemishes born of life's game
Excavate a pattern with a smatter there and there

A rainbow trickles from collar to breast
Tickling still skin while galvanising the rest
Threaten and expose new bones with epic bluster
Re-pose and shuffle gladly to guide the moon upon a bolster

A rainbow trickles around my heart
Beating colours splash a violet start
High and wide and tall and broad
Blooming from boulders broiled with kisses and fraud

A rainbow trickles to my core
To the depths of my womb through a cave filled with gore
Tugging and teasing, it delves down of a frenzy
Excavating my plot engraved with quivering envy

As I breathe deep the trickle becomes a steam
Rainbows run up the length of me
Blistered and beautiful boldly hiking my insides
Fingers kneading, gripping, stroking, singing,
Reminding me that all is in line

As We Turn

When all is cold and lost in pity
A breath of pause helps open our city
Focused in broad daylight now
It was easy to hide in a rumour

Dancing with tree roots reached out to hug
Playing with this earthly drug
No lock is needed as we turn
And turn and turn

Entrenched in this flair with a vacant stare
Dismay at the night's harsh, brash, cold fright
Lacklustre froze in a creeping vice
We are dauntlessly mustered to shine out bright

Only Flow

Float high
Whip cracks on sky
Aloof
Uncouth
There is no truth

Folklore and magic
Classic antics born frantic
A story
Deep quarry
There is no glory

Ring the bell
Ask for meaning to sell
An array
DNA
There is no they

Falling on feet
Here's the meaning you seek
We flew
Eschew
There is only you

Stretch out in time
Not fooled by the feel of two
Sow
And know
There is forever only flow